From Ch[...]ville
Baltons —
Jean
Oct, '99

And on to Loein & René
from Oma Mokey
Enjoy!

Best wishes,
Robert R. Taylor

# THE
# Great Gray Owl

## ON SILENT WINGS

PHOTOGRAPHY AND TEXT BY ROBERT R. TAYLOR

WINDERMERE HOUSE PUBLISHING

Published by Robert R. Taylor
Windermere House Publishing
944 Windermere Ave.
Winnipeg, Manitoba,
Canada, R3T 1A1
Tel: (204) 453-8337

ISBN: 1-55056-502-8

First Edition
Copyright 1997 - Robert R. Taylor

Photography and text by Robert R. Taylor
Book design by Steve Penner

Printed and bound in Canada
by Friesens Corporation
Altona, Manitoba, Canada
ROG OBO

**Windermere House** publications are
available for bulk corporate and
institutional sales, for conferences, business
promotions, customer appreciations, etc.

Inquiries should be directed to the
Corporate Sales Department,
Windermere House Publishing
944 Windermere Avenue
Winnipeg, Manitoba, Canada
R3T 1A1

Dealer inquires are invited.

# DEDICATION

*"The Great Gray Owl – On Silent Wings"* is dedicated
to the memory of my parents, Ross and Alice Taylor,
who always encouraged and supported my interests
in nature and in art.

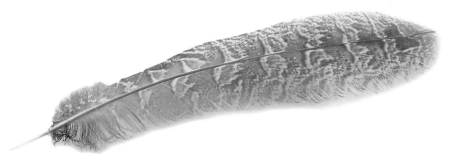

# ACKNOWLEDGEMENTS

I have made a lot of good friends through my interest in natural history and through owls in particular. As a youth, my pals Ted Warren and Jerry Anderson walked many miles with me in search of Saw-whet Owls, and to check our numerous nest barrels for Screech Owls. We have maintained those friendships for almost half a century. In recent years Jerry has worked with me, photographing owls in the winter and at their nests. His help in hauling the photographic towers and other heavy equipment in and out of bogs, usually in cold knee-deep water, is especially appreciated.

Many of the old-time naturalists and scientists helped the three of us with our interest in birds. Frank Smith and Gordon Lambert often included us on their owl banding excursions. Ilmar Talvila, group leader at the Toronto Junior Field Naturalists, encouraged our interest in birding and is still a close friend. Jim Baillie and Terry Shortt of the Royal Ontario Museum in Toronto always found time to share their knowledge with me and included me in many field trips. Reginald James of Willowdale, Ontario, helped me considerably with my observations of Screech Owls, as did Dr. David Hussell during his first years in Canada.

Bill Carrick of Toronto and Dalton Muir of Ottawa were the two most influential friends in directing my career towards nature photography. They employed me to assist them in making wildlife films when I was a teenager and they are still valued friends to this day. In 1970, Dalton and I collaborated on the making of a film on the Great Gray Owl which still appears on television in many countries around the world.

My direct experiences with Great Gray Owls began in 1968. One spring day we received a phone call at the Manitoba Museum of Man and Nature from a woodcutter, Phil Reader. Phil reported that he had found the nest of a Great Gray Owl just north of his home near The Pas, Manitoba. Two days later, the museum director, Jack Herbert, and I drove five-hundred miles north to see the nest. We were met by Phil Reader and Robert Mitchell, who guided us to the nest site, carried loads of heavy gear through the soggy trail, and helped me to install a sixty-foot tower at the nest. My thanks go to those intrepid companions.

Two weeks later, Dr. Robert W. Nero accompanied me on the second trip to the nest at The Pas. Nero, a distinguished ornithologist, has studied the Great Gray Owl extensively since then and has become the foremost authority on this species in North America. He and his friend, Herb Copland, have now banded, weighed, and measured more than one-thousand Great Gray Owls in their quest for scientific data.

Dr. James R. Duncan, Robert Nero's graduate student, and his dedicated wife Patsy have spent over a decade researching Great Gray Owls in the bogs of Manitoba, northwestern Ontario, and northern Minnesota. Their work on this species continues to this day and will likely be a lifetime endeavour. Jim has reviewed the text and offered much valuable advice to assure the accuracy of the information incorporated into the book.

Steve Penner has produced a strong and elegant design for the book. He is a joy to work with as his creativity is combined with a strong practical sense. Steve has also given me a lot of moral support and encouragement to keep going with this project when I seemed to be having second thoughts about forging ahead. Steve's father, Vic Penner, retired editor of the Red River Valley Echo, has kindly done the editing to assure correctness in the grammar and punctuation. The fine printing and binding were done by Friesens of Altona, Manitoba. My particular thanks to David G. Friesen and his highly professional staff.

Two other close friends, Dave Dyson and Peter Sawatzky, have spent many days working in the field with me. Their help was appreciated on some of those cold winter days as we searched for, and tried to photograph, Great Gray Owls.

There are countless others whose friendship, assistance, and knowledge have been a valuable part of my experience and whose encouragement has kept me going toward the completion of this project. It is impossible to mention them all by name, but they are all important and appreciated. My sincere thanks to all who have helped me along the way.

# INTRODUCTION

It is a very special priviledge to be able to share in the private lives of wild creatures. Respectfully, I entered the domain of the Great Gray Owl and began a long and interesting friendship with these fascinating denizens of the northern forest.

As a guest in their world I made every effort to become an integral part of the scene so that they would go about their daily activities in a normal manner. So complete was my acceptance by some pairs, that intimate observations could be made and photographed from a distance of only a few feet. At one ncst, in the mid-seventies, the female would actually allow me to scratch her head as she patiently attended to her duties. Such a rapport was developed through great patience and trust.

My experiences with the Great Gray Owl are truly one of the highlights of my interesting career. I hope that the photographs and text contained within these pages will transport you into the private realm of these magnificent birds.

# FOREWORD

"Mysterious" and "elusive" are words which have often been used to describe the Great Gray Owl. They are indeed difficult to find most of the time as they live the majority of their lives within the expansive northern forest.

This is land which is difficult to traverse and usually remote to humans, but the broad rounded wings of the Great Gray Owls can carry them through this habitat with ease. "On Silent Wings" was chosen for the title because of the impression of stealth that the silent flight of these large owls has made upon the author. Soft edges, as well as a fuzzy upper surface on each of the flight feathers, allows them to move upon each other without creating a rubbing sound when the owls are flying. It is this characteristic which allows them to appear and disappear without notice, in phantom-like fashion.

Great Gray Owls are totally dependent on mouse populations. When prey supplies dwindle in a given area they are obliged to wander in search of food. At such times they may move south into rural and urban areas, where they are more readily seen by birders and others. These so-called invasions occassionally result in high mortality of the owls due to collisions with automobiles, inability to secure sufficient food, and other factors. When they find a good food supply, such movements are their salvation.

Under normal circumstances, they would spend most of the year in the northern forest, adjacent mixed forest, and marginal farmland areas. They are well equipped for survival under cold conditions and for hunting in deep, soft snow.

When they survive the winter and enter into the spring in good health, they will seek out a suitable nest site in an appropriate habitat. As they are unable to build their own nests, they must find an abandoned nest of another species such as a Raven or Goshawk. They will readily use an artificial nest that has been constructed in suitable habitat by naturalists.

It is a special moment when one observes a Great Gray Owl at any time of the year, but to see that big rounded head rising above the edge of a nest in April or May is always a particular thrill.

The populations which inspired this book are those of the northern forests of Canada and northern Minnesota. The Great Gray Owls which reside in the northwestern states have somewhat different diets and habitat preferences. The Lapp Owl of northern Europe and Russia is the same species, though with different plumage charactersitics and usually a more aggressive temperament.

*The Great Gray Owl: On Silent Wings* has been written to carry its readers into the private and intimate world of these intriguing birds. The photographs, though representing many different birds over a time period of three decades, have been selected to illustrate various aspects of the owls' lives and to give visual insight into their world.

# On Silent Wings

*On silent wings*
*The phantom glides.*
*From a favoured perch,*
*Scanning moss and hummock*
*With penetrating ears,*
*The owl descends.*
*An unsuspecting vole*
*Will be captured*
*By lightning talons*
*As the shadowed form*
*Plunges headlong*
*Into the powdery snow.*
*The Great Gray Owl,*
*Which hunts*
*On silent wings.*

# CHAPTER 1

The night sky was filled with stars. The air hung still and crisp at minus forty degrees; nothing moved. Pressed tightly to the trunk of an old gnarled Tamarack, a Great Gray Owl passed the night stoically; eyes closed, but always listening. It was too cold to hunt and the best strategy was to just conserve energy. At regular intervals he would shift from one foot to the other, always pulling the loose foot up into the soft insulating feathers of the breast. It was a long, boring night; one of many.

Hours later, the eastern sky began to lighten. Though he could have hunted effectively in the darkness, he chose to roost overnight. Eventually, hunger pressed him into leaving the relative comfort of his roost to begin wandering the bog in search of food. Hunting wasn't easy during the long winter, but the owl was equipped to make the best of it.

In the half-light of dawn the Great Gray Owl moved from tree to tree; searching; listening. Most of the hunting was done with the ears. The vision could not penetrate the thick mass of snow, but the ears could precisely locate the chewing or squeaking sounds of a small rodent. Nothing was heard.

Several hungry hours later he decided to make his way to the ditches along a nearby road. It was more likely that he would find Meadow Voles along the roadside where it was less boggy and more grassy. The owl was not particular; he just wanted to eat. A few sounds were detected by his sensitive ears and a few unsuccessful hunting forays were made.

Then a persistent chewing sound captured his attention, fully a hundred feet away and beneath more than a foot of snow. His ears locked onto the spot and the sound continued,

triggering a silent direct flight out to the precise site of its origin. The owl hovered briefly in order to fix the location and the timing of the attack; then, with lightning speed he plunged, face-first, into the soft snow. At the last possible instant the feet were thrust forward to punch through the snow and grasp the prey.

Success at last. The Great Gray's foot relaxed as his beak pulled the expiring vole from the razor-sharp talons. Still half buried in snow, he flipped the vole around in his curved beak and swallowed it headfirst.

Having finally procured a meal, the owl was keener than ever to continue the hunt. With his head raised and scanning the area around, he gave a vigorous shake to dislodge the snow which had settled on his back and wings. A strong push with the long feathered legs propelled him into the air and the broad noiseless wings carried the hunter to the top of a nearby stump. The only evidence of the kill was the unique "plunge-hole" which remained in the snow.

A fortnight of minus thirty degree weather seemed as though it would never end. They were days when even the Ravens felt cold. Energy was conserved as much as possible, but still it was necessary to hunt.

There was no crust on the snow and it was too cold to compact significantly, thus offering ideal conditions for the "snow-plunging" method of hunting. From a suitable perch the owl listened intently for the sounds of voles chewing or squeaking beneath the snow. Each listening post was attended patiently until he would decide to move on to a new location.

On sunny days the glare from the snow was intense, causing the Gray Owl to close its eyes much of the time. But the ears were always keen and not even the slightest sound escaped the notice of the observant owl. The ears of the Great Gray Owl, as with other owls, are

extremely sensitive. Stiff, curved feathers behind the facial discs form compact scoop-like structures which direct the sound to the actual ear openings. The facial feathers themselves are more filamentous than others, thus allowing the sound to pass through easily. These features, combined with offset ear openings, enable the owls to locate sound with pinpoint accuracy.

The long breast feathers covered the feet and the fine bristles alongside the beak were adorned with a light coating of frost. Thankfully there was no wind and despite the severe cold the owl was really quite comfortable.

The apparent relaxed mode was abruptly punctuated by strong chewing sounds from beneath the blanket of snow and all of the owl's senses came to full alert. In a matter of seconds the Great Gray Owl departed from a bent spruce top and glided out to investigate the enticing sound. Within a few hovering wingbeats he tipped forward and plunged headlong into the soft snow.

His closed feet punched downward, then extended to reach blindly for the unsuspecting prey. This time, the catch was transferred to the beak and raised to the surface. The hunter carried his quarry to a nearby stump, where the meal was quickly consumed.

Voles spend most of the winter beneath the blanket of snow, but occasionally they will emerge from their tunnels and scamper across the surface. On a calm day in

late winter, as the owl was scanning a grassy meadow, just such an event took place. The eyes of the Great Gray Owl fixed upon the fleeting vole and he launched himself into a long descending glide towards it.

As he neared the target, a dark flash passed in front of him and seized the vole with lightning speed. A Northern Hawk Owl had also seen the quarry from a lofty perch nearby. With its superior speed and dexterity it snatched a meal right in front of the approaching Great Gray. The larger owl circled back to the edge of the woods and resumed his usual hunting technique, while the Hawk Owl perched atop a silvered spire and consumed its prize.

Hunting was good throughout the deep cold of winter, and, in this region at least, the owls remained in good health. Now that the temperatures had moderated somewhat, the owl could sit and absorb the radiant heat from the afternoon sun for brief intervals. Near the horizon, ice crystals hanging in the air gave rise to a magnificent display of "sundogs". These brilliances flanked the sun for barely half an hour, then dipped below the western horizon as did the sun itself.

# CHAPTER 2

The owl's life is mostly a solitary existence during the winter months. It is difficult enough to get a supply of food without having to compete with other owls. Sometimes, it becomes necessary to wander throughout the winter in search of the required sustenance.

A heavy accumulation of snow in the forest and along the roadside ditches, forced the old male Great Gray Owl to move out to the marginal farmlands where the hunting proved to be considerably better. There were groves of Aspens, low swales with Willows, and uncultivated meadows, all of which were great homes for voles. And there were lots of decaying haybales and abandoned buildings, which also favoured mice and voles. When one area proved insufficient, the owl moved on to another.

Many owls found themselves in the same situation and they too were moving about the countryside. Chance encounters brought them together on occasion, but it was not a time for social interaction, so they usually moved away from each other. This was a time for serious hunting, unless the weather interfered.

The old male could be found sometimes sitting atop the Willows, in the lower branches of an Aspen, or on the roof of a derelict barn. He even used the old weathered fenceposts and power poles as hunting perches. This territory became familiar to him in a short time. Though it was cold, most of the days were fairly pleasant. Sunny days, with little or no wind, could be quite tolerable, but there were some days of fierce winds.

On just such a day, the owl could only seek shelter on the leeward side of an Aspen grove and sit tight. All of his feathers were fluffed up to maximize their insulating value. Even the feathers of his face were raised and pushed forward to shield the squinting eyes and the protruding bill. He didn't look much like the efficient hunting machine that was his usual character, and he wasn't much interested in moving from that sheltered perch either. A clear sky overhead indicated that the air was very cold.

The wind howled for most of the day and throughout the night. By dawn of the next day it had tapered off to a stiff breeze and the owl activated his hunting skills. He still sought the sheltered areas as much as possible, perhaps because it was easier to listen or maybe it was just for the comfort. By the middle of the day the air was almost calm and the sun radiated a warmth that was absorbed by the dark plumage of the owl and was most welcomed.

February progressed. As the days lengthened and the temperatures began to moderate, a new problem presented itself to the owl. Heavy clouds moved in from the west, accompanied by warmer temperatures and freezing rain. The precipitation only lasted for about an hour, but it was enough to glaze the surface of the snow with a tough icy shield. The land sparkled in the late sun with a golden sheen that silvered at nightfall. In the coolness of the night the crust hardened.

Though the Great Gray Owl could still punch through this thin barrier in his plunges, he was not nearly as efficient as he had been before the rain. And perhaps it interfered somewhat with hearing the voles beneath the snow. Nevertheless, he persisted, and winter dragged on.

By the end of February, the worst of the winter had passed and early March brought some days that were almost balmy. A few times, the owl hunted by flying low over a meadow or along a row of shrubs with a slow "butterfly-like" flight, all the while peering downward at the ground below. He appeared to be listening for prey as he passed overhead. With a pause and a moment of hovering, a plunge to the ground below sometimes yielded a reward. This was not the usual hunting method, but it obviously held a measure of success.

Eventually, the glazed crust deteriorated and its inconvenience no longer had an effect. Upon the ground, the blanket of snow began to settle and compress as warmer days followed. The radiant sun caused some evaporation and changed the texture of the snow, and now the end of winter was in sight. Eventually, the old male began to wander back toward his favourite bog, though it still was some distance away.

As the massive wings lifted the owl from a "plunge-hole" in the granular snow of early March, a couple of breast feathers came loose and settled on the sparkling surface. As silently as the owl itself, a Gray Jay descended from the forest edge, collected the delicate treasures and disappeared into the bush. They were a precious commodity for lining a newly-built nest.

The jays often crossed paths with the hunting owl; perhaps more of its downy feathers would find their way into the snug little nest carefully hidden in the snow-laden branches of a compact spruce.

Despite the long trip back, the male hunted successfully and still found time and energy to offer communications to other owls that might be within hearing range. Sporadically at first, but building into a nightly routine, he would find a comfortable perch and project his mellow "hooting" into the atmosphere. It was usually a series of several "whoo-whoo-whoo-whoo-whoo-hoo-hoo" sounds with slight punctuation, beginning strong and softening slightly toward the end. He repeated this regularly throughout the nights and more frequently as April approached.

Near the beginning of April, on a clear, calm evening his calling generated a reply. It was weak at first; far away. Then, as the quarter moon lifted above the Spruce tops, the response came booming through the bog from only a short distance off to the east.

A larger, female owl had heard his vocal offerings and had decided to come by to make his acquaintance. It was a cautious approach, a ritual governed by established behaviours of the species. Any interaction of these owls had its procedures, whether it was to lead to courtship or merely a social interaction. That's how it was, on a particular spring evening with faint moonlight reflecting from the eroding snow.

The territorial calls of the male transformed into a variety of soft welcoming notes which were willingly returned by the female. An intimate conversation ensued and a mutual tolerance was the result. Subsequent days found the two owls sharing a hunting territory and communicating on a regular basis.

Their hunting forays covered a fairly large range. On one bright, mild evening the female discovered an old nest near the top of a leaning Tamarack. It still contained a large, rounded mass of compacted snow.

The old nest was built by a pair of Goshawks a few years before. The owls could not carry the sticks to build a nest themselves, so it was always necessary to find a suitable site which was no longer used by its original occupants. This particular nest was in an ideal location and it was still strong and stable.

# CHAPTER 3

In the mysterious hours of twilight the owls became more vigorous and their patience lessened as they moved through the forest on their feeding excursions. Each listening post would serve for only a few minutes before they would move on to the next. Perhaps in this milder weather it was not as important to conserve energy. Maybe this was a better way to hunt as the snow melted and exposed the once safe runways of the voles. Or was there another reason for this restlessness?

On a fresh invigorating night, one which could have inspired poets, most of the forest inhabitants were obliged to signal their presence. Sound carried through the still air of the bog as if it was meant to reach the horizon. There was even a hint of an echo.

A series of mellow whistles emanated from the mixed forest of a glacial ridge just north of the bog. It repeated, time and again, each time rising to a crescendo and then tapering off. On a horizontal Aspen limb a tiny Boreal Owl shifted his feet, took a deep breath, and projected another love-song into the night air.

In the background, seemingly several miles away, the moaning howl of a wolf briefly silenced the small owl. It was answered by another and then a third. The wolves had no particular purpose to their communication other than just keeping in touch with each other as they wandered randomly. This too was heard by the Great Gray Owls, but was no cause for concern.

They had their own business to attend. A mutual acceptance had grown into a genuine attraction. Their intimate conversation did have purpose and there were behavioural activities prescribed for the occasion.

A fluttering descent to the floor of the bog yielded a plump vole in the grasp of the male. While still standing on the soggy ground he transferred it from the deadly talons to his curved beak so that it could be carried more conveniently and then his soft, ample wings lifted him quietly to a nearby snag. Usually he would consume the acquired meal, but not this time. This was to be a gift.

From the top of this silvered stump the male Great Gray Owl issued a series of three strong and distinct hoots. The prized vole lay at his feet. Out of the darkness came a single call, a blend of hoot and bark. This was the female's response which he had desired.

With the vole firmly grasped in his beak, he leaned forward and launched himself into the blackness. Flaring up onto the branch where the female awaited, he began to call excitedly and she did likewise. There was some bowing and swaying and much anxiety. Amid the fervor of the moment, the vole was presented to the female by her suitor.

It dangled from her beak for a brief time and was then swallowed in a series of quick gulps. The gift was gratefully accepted and acknowledged by an offer to preen the loose head feathers of the male. The following half-hour was spent in mutual preening and soft conversation. Pair-bonding had begun.

Throughout the nights and sometimes during the day the male sounded his series of soft but emphatic hoots; Whoo-whoo- whoo-whoo-whoo-hoo-hoo-hoo, descending in volume towards the end. This was his turf and others might well be informed.

# CHAPTER 4

There were some mild days in April and the night air no longer held the sting of winter. The wind blew occasionally, but mostly there was a gentle promise of spring. Residual snow slowly melted from the old nest in the Tamarack and it was visited with regularity by the pair of Great Gray Owls.

The nest site was scrutinized and was accepted to be their home for the nesting period. The view was excellent, the nest platform was adequate and firm, and there were no major obstructions to flying to and fro. It would do just fine.

Both the male and the female had enjoyed a winter with sufficient food and they were in good health in preparation for raising a family.

The rituals of courtship increased in intensity in early April. Many voles were presented to the female by her amorous mate and much time was spent at the mutual preening activity. For a time the male's overtures were received with casual interest, but eventually the female was receptive and mating was initiated.

Within a few days a rounded, off-white egg was deposited in the nest and the maternal duties began. Even though the clutch was incomplete she would begin to incubate with the laying of the first egg. The other eggs would follow at two-day intervals until there were three. A usual clutch would be three, and in some years a pair of Great Gray Owls might lay four or even five eggs.

Sitting aloft on a platform of sticks and twigs for more than a month must be the ultimate in boredom, but that's what it takes to produce an owl family. Everything started off well. The days were easy and the night skies were crystal clear. The day that the third egg was laid a change came in the weather. Heavy, low cloud moved in from the northwest and the temperature began to drop.

By mid-day a few snowflakes began to fall, and within an hour large, wet flakes covered the rim of the nest and the back of the female. It continued throughout the day and into the night. At regular intervals she would shake the snow from her back and try to settle comfortably back onto the eggs. As the night pressed on it became almost impossible for her to stay dry and to conserve her body heat so that it could be directed towards her eggs. Somehow she managed. When dawn came to the bog that morning the ground was covered in fresh snow, the trees were also dressed in white, and the owl was mantled in this late reminder of the past winter.

The male had taken shelter under the heavy branches of a nearby Spruce, where he could keep an eye on the nest and issue a reassuring call every now and then. He did not hunt that night.

The sky cleared before dawn. By mid-morning the April sun eroded the fresh snow from the upper branches and eventually cleared the decorative blanket from most of the drooping limbs. The attentive female busied herself by removing snow from the nest and putting her feathers in order. At daybreak the male went off to begin hunting but had not yet returned.

Morning hours in the forest set the stage for new bird songs, some of which had not been heard since the previous summer. Overhead, a Common Snipe toured the sky and with each descent, air whistled through the thin outer feathers of the snipe's fanned tail and created that characteristic "winnowing" sound. It was reminiscent of the Boreal Owl's calling earlier in the year, though considerably weaker.

A Pileated Woodpecker passed through the area one day, announcing its presence with the typical loud staccato notes, then disappeared off to the northeast. Meanwhile, the thin whistle of the Black-capped Chickadee became a resident sound. Ravens regularly issued their gutteral calls as they passed by in the sky above.

None of these sounds were missed by the ever-alert ears of the Great Gray Owl female as she sat dutifully upon her eggs. Even as she dozed in the warmth of the afternoon sun she was not unaware of the neighbourhood activities. Often she would stare skyward to watch a bird fly overhead, so high that it would not be seen by most eyes. But her eyes were extraordinary, very powerful and well tuned.

She left the nest only twice each day. During the morning she would sometimes fly to a nearby perch, always within sight of the nest, then stretch and preen for a few minutes before returning. By late afternoon or early evening she was ready for another short break. Never did she go far away or stay off the eggs for very long. Her attachment to that clutch of eggs was strong, and it grew stronger with each passing day.

The roles of the two sexes were clearly defined. Her job was to incubate the eggs, tend to the nest, and feed the young owls. The male was obliged to provide the food for her and for himself, and eventually for the owlets. Both parents would attempt to protect the nest contents from predators or intruders if the need arose.

Hunting was much easier now than in the depths of winter. There were more small rodents to be had and they were more accessible. So with regularity he would arrive at the edge of the nest carrying a food offering for his mate. As for his own needs, they too were filled. And still he had time to continue his territorial calling and those less obvious sounds which served to strengthen the bonds between him and his partner.

# CHAPTER 5

Spring is a time of increased activity in the natural world, and the bog was no exception. As the first pools of melt-water formed between the hummocks of Sedge and Sphagnum Moss, the clucking calls of Wood Frogs and the creaking sounds of Boreal Chorus Frogs began. Sitting in a puddle of ice-water could hardly be inspirational, nevertheless their songs rattled in the ears of the Great Gray Owls. Gray Tree Frogs soon added their calls to the ensemble.

The first White-throated Sparrow song echoed through the bog in mid-April. In a few days they seemed to be everywhere, piping their thin melodic whistles to claim a territory and hopefully to attract a mate.

Tiny bits of green began to appear on the Tamarack buds as the bog brightened from the muted tones of winter to the lively hues of spring. Soon the buds burst forth into delicate green sprays of fresh needles and the nest site took on a new beauty. The owl raised her body and reached down to turn her eggs.

Spring progressed. Soon various types of warblers sang their melodious songs amid the freshened vegetation. The wispy notes of a Black and White Warbler competed for attention with those of a Redstart. A Palm Warbler wagged its tail under the low canopy of Labrador Tea. Strongest of all the bird sounds was that of a Connecticut Warbler. The melodious, lower-pitched song moved around the bog in an unsettled manner. From the very tip of a ragged Black Spruce, a tiny Ruby-crowned Kinglet sang incessantly. Such a vigorous song from a diminutive bird seemed hardly possible. Another impressive songster was the Winter Wren.

Its long and intricate vocalization was issued at regular intervals from a favourite lichen-covered stump. A profusion of brilliant yellow Marsh Marigolds accented the ground below.

A few less obvious, but equally important, songs filtered through the background chorus. The wispy call of a Yellow-bellied Flycatcher could almost be missed, except by another of the same species. A Boreal Chickadee passed by on occasion, as did a lone Red-breasted Nuthatch. Off in the distance somewhere, even an Olive-sided Flycatcher could be heard.

There were other species around of course, but one which was taking up residence near the owl's nest was of particular interest. A pair of Yellow-rumped Warblers searched diligently for insects, pollen, and any other tasty morsel which suited their diet. While inspecting the branches of a Tamarack one of the warblers discovered a discarded breast feather from the Great Gray Owl which had caught on a twig and was gently wafting in the slight breeze. With all of the enthusiasm of a treasure hunter the warbler wrestled the long, soft feather free from the twig and carried it off to a secret nesting place. Over the next few days several more of the owl feathers were collected by the warblers and incorporated into their nest construction.

It was now the middle of May. High above all of this warbler activity, the female Great Gray Owl patiently incubated her precious eggs. The past month had been pretty routine for the most part. Her mate had provided well for her as she sat on the nest around the clock for thirty days, but all that was about to change.

For the last couple of days she had heard sounds coming from inside one of the eggs. It was a high-pitched twitter; sometimes strong, sometimes faint. Her attachment to the nest and her eggs became even stronger. On this morning she could also hear a weak scratching sound, then a small crack appeared in the shell. As the morning progressed, a triangular chip of the eggshell fell away revealing the tiny beak of a hatching owl. The bright, white egg tooth had worn through the tough membrane and through the stiff outer casing. The critical part was now as the chick must continue to release itself from the egg before the membrane dries out and becomes even tougher. The female was anxious, and very attentive.

By noon, the tiny owlet was free and securely tucked beneath the warm breast of its mother, along with the two remaining eggs. Most of the time it slept. In two days the event was repeated. Two days after that the last egg hatched and the nest contained three healthy young of different sizes.

The female now became much more demanding. She called for food incessantly. The male hunted with an intensity never before experienced by him, and he was successful. Throughout the days he would tour the bog, perching and listening, then moving on to do it again. The voles were active and although they mostly travelled through tunnels under the hummocks and runways concealed by vegetation, they would fall victim to the deadly strike of the owl. With each success he would report directly back to the awaiting female.

# CHAPTER 6

The owl's wings were noiseless as he gracefully travelled the unobstructed routes through the bog. Occasionally, with great dexterity, he would tuck in his large wings and pass smoothly through a narrow gap between adjacent trees.

This territory was familiar to him now. He knew every path and perch and he flew it comfortably and efficiently. With a fresh vole securely held in his beak, he once again flowed through the home range toward the anxious calls of the female. His arrival was announced with the usual soft hooting a few seconds before an abrupt landing on the edge of the nest. This time she lunged at him and snatched the vole. There was little of the usual formality; the owlets were begging for food and she had a job to do. He turned and departed immediately.

The nestlings were small and not yet able to cope with a large food item on their own. At this stage, the female was obliged to tear the prey into small bits which she delicately offered to the hungry youngsters. The oldest of the offspring, now seven days and growing rapidly, was the largest and most demanding. As the female dismantled the fresh vole, the eager chick grabbed the remainder of the morsel and tried to swallow it in one piece.

It was a noble attempt. The gaping mouth wrapped around the furry chunk and tried vigorously to choke it down, but it was too much. It was retrieved from the floor of the nest by the female and she resumed her motherly duties. As she continued the patient feeding of the mid-sized owlets the smallest of them slept quietly beneath her breast. When the chores were complete they all drifted off into a light sleep. A Hermit Thrush sang in the distance.

Most days were fairly routine during the raising of the nestlings. The female would feed the youngsters according to their demands and she would always be very attentive. At times, she would preen them gently, tuck them under the warm feathers of her breast when necessary, and even shade them from the sun when required.

She kept the nest as clean as possible. Any pellets or deposits of excrement in the nest were eaten by the female. As the owlets grew older they would back up to the edge of the nest and propel their feces over the side, usually raising their wings over their back for balance.

The weather was variable during the month of May. There were balmy days with light clouds and a gentle breeze, there were hot days without a breath of wind, and there were cool rainy days when everything felt soggy. The owls were out there in the elements and had to take whatever came along.

It rained most of the night after several warm sunny days, and in the morning the forest was shrouded in heavy fog. With her babies snuggled in beneath her, the female owl used her body to protect them from the rain and cold. She was a mess. Though her wing and tail feathers had shed much of the water, her head was bedraggled. Pointed clumps of saturated feathers stuck out in all directions, and, except for the bright yellow eyes, she didn't look much like her usual self.

The fog lifted during the morning and by noon she and her surroundings were beginning to dry out. Much preening was done that day. She hadn't seen the male overnight, but had heard him call several times. In the morning he delivered a fat, warm vole which she had accepted with enthusiasm. Afterwards, he sat on a horizontal limb nearby and gave his territorial hooting call several times before heading off into the foggy woods.

The owlets grew quickly and at the age of nine days the oldest of them could swallow a vole in one piece. It took a bit of work, but when presented with the opportunity it grabbed the prey from the mother's bill, turned it lengthwise, and swallowed the morsel headfirst with a few

laboured gulps. The other youngsters grabbed at the vole but they had no chance of wresting it from their sibling.

In a few days they would all be able to consume their food in the same manner. Wing and tail feathers steadily lengthened and grey body feathers began to dominate the soft white down. Their heads were losing the pointed appearance and were taking on the soft, rounded look characteristic of owls. Waxy sheaths were radiating out around the eyes, indicating the broad face discs that would eventually materialize. The nestlings were looking more like owls with each passing day.

The duties of the female were slightly lessened as the owlets grew. At two to three weeks of age they could eat without her having to dissect the prey, they were able to do most of their own preening, and they could huddle together for warmth. Only when it was cold did she need to brood them.

Now she felt more inclined to leave the nest to attend to her own needs. On a favourite Tamarack snag about thirty feet away she would sit for extended periods, sometimes just watching and sometimes preening. Every few days she would seek out a pool of clear water among the mossy hummocks. With a cautious approach she would land near the water and then walk into it to bathe.

Standing in the pool she would first dip her head into the water and let it run over her head and her back a few times.

This was followed by squatting and fluttering her wings to shower water all over herself and the adjacent vegetation. Droplets of water would fly in all directions, catching the sunlight like an explosion of diamonds emanating from the boggy turf. In a minute or two, the activity subsided and she would fly to a lofty perch to dry off and to preen her laundered plumage. All the while she listened for calls from her nestlings or her mate. She was well aware of her vulnerability while bathing and somewhat anxious about her unprotected youngsters. Soon she returned to the nest.

At three weeks, the wing feathers of the young owls were developed to the point where they could create some resistance to air. For much of the day they would flap their wings vigorously. This strengthened the flight muscles and gave them a new activity to pass the time. The eldest of the owlets would stand at the very edge of the nest and peer over the side. Its wing-flapping was often combined with jumping, up to two or three inches off the platform, a precarious activity indeed.

In the light breeze of a spring day, one of these exercise sessions resulted in the launching of the young owl over the side of the nest. An awkward descent to the ground was buffered by the rapid fluttering of inefficient wings. A crash landing on soft ground left the fledgling somewhat bewildered but without injury of any kind.

After remaining on a mossy hummock for a considerable length of time, the wayward young owl made its way over to an inclined branch and climbed up, using its feet and bill for grasping, and flapping its wings for balance. From this lofty perch, it looked around to survey the surroundings, then dozed off to sleep in the morning sun. A halo of downy feathers glowed in the sunlight.

# CHAPTER 7

A few years earlier, the nesting season had not gone so well for the owls. It had been a long, cold winter and though the voles were well insulated under a heavy blanket of snow their numbers were few when it began. Vole populations fluctuate for a number of reasons. When their numbers are high there is more chance of disease spreading amongst them, greater stress from crowding in their preferred habitats, and sometimes a diminished food supply. Some climatic factors may also affect them, such as inadequate snow cover in the winter to protect them from the cold, or a quick thaw in the spring which may flood their homes and may even cause some of the voles to drown.

During that particular winter, the hunting was so difficult that many of the Great Gray Owls had wandered southward in search of an adequate food supply and more suitable hunting conditions. Many of them ended up far south of the boreal forest, often in open farm country and even on the edge of urban areas.

A whole new set of hazards face the owls when such movements become necessary. Aside from the prospect of starvation, they are at greater risk of colliding with motor vehicles and wires. Although humans are more appreciative of such creatures now than in the past, there are still those who would shoot the approachable and unsuspecting owls. Great Horned Owls are a significant predator on the Great Grays and as the Great Gray Owls move southward they run a greater risk of encountering these fearsome foes. Many of the wandering owls fail to return to their home range at the end of winter.

Those Great Gray Owls which do make it through a severe winter will instinctively seek a suitable nesting territory and a partner and will make an attempt at nesting. The pair which occupied the Tamarack bog that spring began with all of the vigour and optimism of a healthy pair in an abundant year.

The nest was selected and the territory claimed in the usual manner. Courtship and mating proceeded normally, but the female produced only two eggs instead of the usual three. With her clutch completed, she dutifully sat and incubated the precious eggs for the required thirty days. It was a long and tedious period, punctuated by intervals of egg-turning, brief departures from the nest to preen and stretch, and by deliveries of food from her mate.

Attentively she sat, day after day, managing her eggs and guarding her nest. Her own needs were secondary but still they were important. As hunger increased, she would issue her food demand calls more frequently and more emphatically. The male, who provided for both of them, was under great pressure to capture sufficient prey and often had to go far afield to do so. They made it through the incubation period and were rewarded with the hatching of the first egg on a mild, sunny morning in May. Two days later the second egg hatched and the requirement for food began to increase significantly.

All went well for the first week, though the first-hatched seemed to be stronger and growing a little faster than the second. The voles which were provided by the male were carefully dissected by the female and shared among the owlets. The first sign of trouble came when the female began to eat part of the voles which were destined for the youngsters. She was not getting enough for herself, and, despite her maternal instincts, her needs must prevail.

At the age of nine days the smallest chick expired. Whether it was eaten or simply removed from the nest is unknown, but only one owlet remained in the nest.

The surviving owlet seemed to be doing well, increasing in size and vigour. Frequent calls from the female indicated that she was hungry and that she wanted the male to bring more food, but the male was having a difficult time catching enough. So emphatic and repetitious were her demands that they attracted the attention of a Black Bear. The opportunistic bear watched for a while, then proceeded to climb up the nest tree.

The protective mother hooted a warning, arched her wings, and raised her feathers in defiance of the approaching bear. The tree wavered and flakes of bark tumbled to the ground as the awkward bear neared the nest. By this time the frantic female had retreated to a nearby branch and was punctuating her warning calls with loud snapping sounds from her bill.

Her efforts to deter the bear were all in vain. With the nestling reared back at the far edge of the nest, and it too snapping its bill in defiance, the bear cuffed the owlet with a swift and deadly blow. Clumsily, the marauder backed down the scarred trunk and retrieved the remains of the baby owl.

Traumatized by the event, the female Great Gray Owl continued her protest as she followed the departing bear through the bog for a short distance. The nest platform drew her back. Upon the nest she stood and stared at the empty mass of twigs and rubble. A season which had started with so much promise now ended in failure. The male would soon return to discover the disaster.

# CHAPTER 8

Sitting on a branch all day waiting for the next delivery of food could be quite boring were it not for the inquisitive nature of the fledglings and the constant activities of the neighbours. Alertness is one of the keys to survival and the young eyes of the owlets missed few movements within their range.

Even as they dozed in the afternoon sun, their ears were tuned to the slightest sounds. Though lacking the large facial discs of adults, the offset ear openings could still locate faint noises with some accuracy. So it was, with much turning, tilting, and bobbing of the heads that the fledglings would pass the days in amusement and all the while they were sharpening their perceptive skills.

At regular intervals, more frequently when hungry, they would issue an emphatic call which would keep them in touch with their siblings and enable the parents to locate them when bringing food. This call, a short and somewhat raspy emanation, had great penetrating power and would carry through the forest for some distance.

The owlets were prone to wandering. Their restless wings, though only developed to half of their potential length, could carry them safely to the ground a stone's throw away when the urge came to move. Having descended safely, though often clumsily, they would rest awhile and look around for an angled tree or log. Using their beak in similar fashion to a parrot, grasping with their sharp talons and flapping their wings for balance, the young owls could easily climb an inclined trunk to gain elevation.

During the course of a day this combination of climbing up and fluttering down could transport the owlets a significant distance through the bog. Thus, the importance of the contact or locating calls is obvious.

By now, both adults would be actively hunting though the female would not range far from the youngsters. It was still her role to collect the prey from the male and to make the deliveries to the owlets herself, but now this procedure was not so strictly enforced. A soft hoot, repeated two or three times, would announce the offering. The demand, the most vigorous call from a fledgling, usually determined who would get fed.

It is imperative that the adults capture enough prey to satisfy their offspring if they are all to survive. But it is even more important that the parents keep themselves in good shape or the helpless youngsters have no hope for maturing. Thus the owls must not only capture two or three voles a day per owlet, but also three or four per day for each of themselves.

As the season wears on, the vole population within the home range may become somewhat depleted. This can happen despite the fact that the voles are raising families of their own beneath the hummocks. If hunting becomes too difficult in the home range, the owls will be forced to move into fresh territory. Keeping in touch with each other becomes even more important as they begin their summer wanderings.

# CHAPTER 9

In the heat of the afternoon, towering cumulus clouds arose in the western sky. This was not uncommon on a summer day, but these were higher and blacker than usual. The owls looked toward the sky from time to time, but mostly they went about their business as usual.

Thunder rumbled constantly and the light faded. A few sprinkles of rain began to fall as a brilliant flash penetrated the darkness and a simultaneous boom hammered the bog. Within seconds another flash followed, though further away. The concerned female gave a series of calls, to which her fledglings responded instantly. The storm was a new experience for the owlets, but the adults had been through this many times before.

More lightning flashed and heavy rain poured from the somber sky. For a short time the winds grew very strong and blew the rain through the quavering trees with a saturating force. During the winds it was difficult for the owls to hold on to their jostling perches, but all survived and eventually the storm passed. There, in the soggy Tamarack and Spruce, sat five bedraggled owls. Though the wing and tail feathers shed the rain efficiently, their heads and breasts were in total disarray. Often they had shaken their heads to dispel the raindrops, but they got soaked anyway.

The next few hours were spent preening and drying out. The adults soon resumed their quest for sustenance, but even as they sat listening and staring at the ground they would pause to groom or to shake out their feathers. There was little vocalization as the whole family was busy with plumage maintenance.

The evening was calm and peaceful. A few birds sang weak replicas of their full spring songs and the Connecticut Warbler reappeared after a couple of secretive weeks. A Northern Goshawk triggered a few anxious moments as it slipped efficiently through the trees and disappeared toward the west. With the onset of night, the scent of smoke wafted through the forest.

Forest fires can be disastrous to the resident wildlife. Some birds may escape by flying away and some mammals may outrun the fire, but young birds and many of the mammals perish in its path. The vegetation is usually destroyed. Though the owls would not know the significance of the smoke, the prospect was ominous.

The heavy rainfall was localized; some areas got drenched and others just got the lightning. A dry meadow, several miles to the north and west, was ignited by lightning and the accompanying winds had fanned it into a small fire. The flames adavanced across the meadow and into the neighbouring forest and the smoke dispersed across the land.

Fortune smiled upon the forest and its residents that day, for within the first mile the fire intersected with a saturated bog and soon vanished. In its wake, a blackened landscape smouldered throughout the night.

# CHAPTER 10

All activity of the owls came to a stop on a sweltering hot July afternoon. With drooping wings and open beaks, adults and young alike were panting rapidly to cool themselves. Even in the shaded bog the temperature and humidity discouraged any attempt to search for food or even to move.

Deer flies and the larger "Bulldogs" annoyed the owls constantly but were seldom able to land on them long enough to bite. Black flies were a different story altogether. They would seek out the more radiant parts of the owls, around the eyes and at the base of the beak. Areas unprotected by feathers were vulnerable to the persistent black flies during the daytime and to voracious mosquitoes at dusk and throughout the night.

At least at night the air cooled somewhat, giving the owls a measure of relief from the uncomfortable heat of the day. The fledglings had grown considerably and were now able to make sustained, though inefficient, flights. But still the adults must provide their meals.

As July flowed into August the young owls grew as large as the parents. Now they were competent enough to keep up with the adults on their foraging trips through the bog. And now they were learning how to hunt. It would be a few weeks yet before they mastered the intricacies of successful hunting and there would be many blundered attacks, but they would eventually become proficient. If not, they would be short lived. The parents could not sustain them forever.

The nights were cooler in August, and longer with each passing day. Most traces of the downy fledgling plumage had vanished. The flight feathers were now as large as those of the adults, perhaps even slightly larger, and the tails were now grown to full length. To all intents and purposes those awkward, dependent owlets were now grown up. The tips of their tail feathers were still pointed where the down had been attached a few short weeks ago. Except for

a few details, such as the facial disk which is slower to fill out, they now looked like full-fledged Great Gray Owls. Independence crept closer each day.

Flies and mosquitoes pestered them less and less. Bird songs were now infrequent and some songbirds had begun to move southwards. The colourful warblers of spring were now drab as were their young; more cryptic, less vulnerable to predators. They need not worry about the Great Gray Owls; they are not fast enough to catch a warbler and lack the needed agility. Gray Owls are built for catching small mammals, mostly voles. In that niche they are very efficient.

August dragged on, and soon it was September. Though the days were still warm, the nights became quite cool. The green began to recede from deciduous leaves, revealing the reds and yellows of autumn. One by one the young owls wandered off and lost touch with their siblings and their parents. Now they must fend for themselves. It would not be easy, and there were still many lessons to be learned. The first year of life for most birds is filled with hazards.

# CHAPTER 11

Bright colours of autumn signal the transition into another season. Sedges and grasses across the bog and in the nearby meadows took on a variety of golden hues, while accents of red were provided by leaves on the Dogwood and other shrubbery. The youthful owlets gained experience with each passing day; experience which would be crucial to surviving their first winter.

Many times they would intently watch a leaf descend to the ground, intrigued by its movement, then puzzled by its stillness. They were learning to be more observant, with the eyes and the ears, and they were learning to be patient. Throughout those early days of independence they had made many unsuccessful attempts to secure a vole from the maze of hummocks, deadfall, and Labrador Tea. Somehow, they always managed to get enough sustenance to keep them going, though there were lean days.

A new sound interrupted the concentration of one of the owls as it listened for its next meal. Soft thumps occurred at regular intervals; something was falling from the trees. High in the conifers a Red Squirrel was severing cone-laden twigs and dropping them to the floor of the bog. There was an urgency to its work as there is to all Red Squirrel activities. Later, the squirrel would collect and store the cones in a "midden" to serve as a winter food supply. All of this was only of casual interest to the owl, as they don't normally eat squirrels.

Daylight hours diminished until they were equalled by those of darkness, and then surpassed. The air cooled and at night there was a hint of frost. The fine needles of the Tamaracks soon yellowed and began to detach and tumble to the floor of the bog. Only a few sounds penetrated the still air. A wandering Raven, a local Gray Jay, a Three-toed Woodpecker, and a small band of Boreal Chickadees signalled their presence.

A number of mammals rambled about the forest. A weasel searched out those same voles on which the owls rely and an old Black Bear scouted around for a place to bed down for the winter. From the direction of an open meadow the young owls could hear the rustling of vegetation punctuated by the occasional snapping of a twig. Their attention was fixed upon the approaching sounds as a large bull Moose came into view. With great curiousity they watched the massive, antlered animal pass by and one of them nervously snapped its bill a couple of times. The Moose turned an ear toward the owl but never even looked up.

There were a few active Moose trails in the region and no doubt the owls observed them sporadically. On many nights the mellow, haunting tones of wolves reached out to each other over their large territory. These sounds are a part of the owl's world and soon became familiar.

The owlets had travelled a long way from the nest site by this time. They hadn't seen or heard the parents for several days and only a couple of times did they cross paths with each other. They still issued their food demand calls occasionally when they were hungry, but to no avail. They were on their own now and must rely on their own skills.

Silence is an element of efficiency for hunting owls, as is stillness and concentration. One of the young owls found it difficult to listen due to the constant chatter of a nervous Red Squirrel. It leaned forward, gave a gentle shake, and moved on to a quieter part of the bog. While perched upon an old twisted stump adorned with lichens and silvered with age, the young Great Gray Owl stared at the ground as a Red-backed Vole scurried from one hummock to another and disappeared. A return trip would be its undoing.

Autumn in the northern forest was fresh and invigorating. There were no flies and mosquitoes to pester the young owls and the bird songs of the summer no longer filled the forest air. Despite a few distractions, the hunting was good and they managed to procure enough food to keep them healthy. Their survival skills served them well.

As the season progressed, most of the leaves came to rest upon the ground and began the long slow process of decaying back into soil. The days shortened and a heavy, grey October sky brought the first flurries of snow.

# CHAPTER 12

The adolescent owls, now in their sixth month, gained competence with each passing day. The eldest of the three had roamed a long way to the south and had discovered an abandoned farmstead. It was a good hunting place, as the unworked fields and weathered buildings supported a heavy population of Meadow Voles.

Silvered fenceposts, abandoned implements, decrepit sheds, and even the old outhouse provided ideal perches from which to listen and scan for the voles. It was a peaceful place, visited on occasion by a lone Coyote who came for a share of the voles, and who would sometimes shatter the silence with a series of yelps and howls. The owl might respond with a couple of soft hoots, or perhaps just sit and watch.

Each day at dusk, from beneath the back porch of the old farmhouse, a strange animal would appear and begin to forage around the property. The owl had never seen anything like this: it waddled more than walked, and it stopped to investigate almost everything. It was black with two white stripes along the back to the bushy tail. Curiously the owl watched, but it was too large to eat.

Great Gray Owls are programmed for hunting voles and mice. Rarely do they attempt to capture anything else. They might catch a few Wood Frogs in spring or some other small item that presents itself, but their diet is very restricted, as is their ability to secure it.

It is not surprising then, that young the owl lingered about the old farm for several weeks. The hunting was easy and the supply constant. The siblings were probably still in the forest somewhere. Most likely the adult female had abandoned the male and the young by this time, and had gone off on her own. The male might still be on the home range, though he could be anywhere by now.

Most of the nights were cold and clear and millions of stars spread across the sky. The owl moved around the farmstead from one favourite perch to another. Some vantage points were higher than others, some were more productive, and some more comfortable. The old birdhouse, high on a pole at the corner of the yard, provided a view of most of the clearing. On windless days, it was an integral part of the circuit. During the twilight hours, lower posts were preferred. Perhaps the owl felt less vulnerable nearer the ground, or maybe it was just a better way to hunt.

Though the owl could see well during the darkened hours, the ears were still the primary sense used to locate the voles. The old fenceposts were ideal for listening. If unsuccessful after a reasonable period of time, the owl could simply move along to another post and so on down the line.

Due to the generous supply of food, the owl was in good condition. In the early part of November there was a significant drop in temperature and many days of heavy cloud. No longer did the sun warm the air by day, and the days were short.

Late one afternoon, large flakes of snow began to fall from the dark grey sky. Before long, a skiff of snow covered the ground and still it continued. The weathered tops of the fenceposts were capped with soft white mounds except for the one where the owl remained. Snowflakes destined for this post settled upon the head and back of the motionless bird. The long bristles alongside its beak collected an assortment of geometric crystals as did the lashes above its squinting eyes. A vigorous shake dislodged most of them but more soon followed.

Though not uncomfortable in the fresh snow, the owl decided to head for the shelter of the adjacent woods. This was a new experience, one which would play a major role in the life of the owl.

# CHAPTER 13

A layer of snow settled on the ground and silenced the rustling of fallen leaves. As the light of a November moon reflected from the crystalline surface it became easier for the owls to see, but hearing became more difficult. For the past month or so they were aided in their hunting by the crispness of the ground cover as the voles shuffled about.

Now the place was soggy and decorated with a thin white blanket. The forest was still and peaceful on this windless night. There was no particular need for the owls to call in winter, though they did issue a single hoot at times. Vocalization could serve to connect with others of the species which might be nearby, but for the most part it was a solitary existence.

The local wolves were now defining their winter trails and marking their territory. Often at night they would join in chorus to advise each other of their location. Sometimes they seemed to sing for the pure joy of doing so and the bog would come alive with their eerie tones.

The scrawny tips of Black Spruce speared the moonlit sky, interspersed with the delicate silhouettes of Tamarack. Starlight filtered through the atmoshere and settled amongst the darkened trees. A shadowed form hunched over on a lower branch and sat motionless with its large round head directed toward the ground. Abruptly, it dropped like a giant fluttering moth and scattered the fresh snowflakes. In its grip a small rodent expired.

This drama would be repeated often in the days to come. The rhythms and cycles of nature are intricate and well established. By night and by day, voles must perish so that owls might live. Its meal consumed, the owl lifted quietly from among the hummocks and settled on a broken snag. From this new post the listening continued as the moon descended in the western sky.

There are nights when all of nature seems at peace. The air is calm, the sky is clear, and the creatures of the forest go about their business under the cloak of darkness.

A filagree of branches, black and crisp, decorates the foreground while overhead the northern lights waft gently across the sky like a huge gossamer curtain. The "big dipper" tilts as if to spill its imaginary contents into the black expanse, and stars fill the space between horizons until obscured by the inky spires of earthbound Spruce.

# CHAPTER 14

Winter arrived in a subtle manner. There were days of light snow flurries, sunny days that still provided a measure of radiant heat, then a gradual drop in temperatures and a steady accumulation of snow.

December flowed into January, and soon the owls were living in the depths of winter. For the young of the year it was a new experience; for the adults it was another winter to test their endurance. All had scattered by this time, away from their summer territory, in search of lucrative hunting grounds. They patrolled roadsides, farmlands, and different types of forest. They went where they had to in order to survive.

Always they had to balance their activities between catching their life-giving prey and conserving their precious energy. The extreme cold was not a significant problem as long as food was plentiful and the wind didn't get too strong.

Wind is an enemy of this wintering owl. On a calm day the thick layer of downy feathers insulates the body and reduces heat loss. On a windy day, not only is the heat taken away faster by the moving air, but the ruffling of the feathers reduces the effectiveness of the protective layer. That a bird survives these northern winters at all is somewhat miraculous.

Windy days are best spent within the confines of the forest. Calm days might well find the owls in very exposed locations such as a marsh, a roadside, or a farm field. Fresh "plunge-holes" in the snow give evidence of their hunting.

Winter days are not all bleak and uncomfortable. Many of them, in fact, are quite pleasant. On sunny days of relative calm, the owls can hunt in a leisurely, though persistent, manner. The silhouette of a hunting owl against a colourful winter sunset is a memorable sight indeed.

# CHAPTER 15

The forest is silent now. No longer does the resonant hooting of the owl penetrate its depths. The stage is set for a new drama, but where are the actors?

Last year's nest sits empty, high above the flooded bog. Melt-water from the heavy snow fills the once active vole tunnels and covers many of the hummocks. Where there is no food, there can be no owls.

The forced winter wanderings of the Great Gray Owls may have led them to more productive hunting grounds, or perhaps to starvation. Hopefully, they are performing their ritualistic courtships in a distant bog filled with voles.

And what of the youngsters of last season. Were all those foraging trips in vain, or have they survived to continue on in the traditions of Great Gray Owls? Are they now establishing territories in secluded bogs across the north? Have they learned to be good hunters? Will they produce families of their own?

The empty nest sits lifeless, cradled in the awakening branches of the Tamarack. Will the owls ever return? Will it be occupied by a Goshawk, a Raven, or perhaps a Long-eared Owl? Or will it just deteriorate over the years and find its way to the forest floor?

In the stillness of a late winter evening the soft hooting of the Great Gray Owl may someday, once again, waft through the branches of this precious bog. For now it is just a pleasant memory.

# Great Gray Owl

*Old man of the woods,*
*You see more than we realize.*
*From your Tamarack roost*
*You absorb each transient sound*
*And spend your days deep in thought,*
*Or so it appears.*
*Do you possess the wisdom*
*For which we give you credit,*
*Or has your mystique*
*Activated our imagination?*

# THE GREAT GRAY OWL – GENERAL INFORMATION

## DESCRIPTION

The Great Gray Owl *(Strix nebulosa nebulosa)* is the largest of all North American owls. The length of these birds, sitting upright, is from 24 to 30 inches (60 - 76 cm.). Their wingspan ranges from about 53 inches to 60 inches (135 - 152 cm.) and the tail measurement is from 10 to 13 inches (25 - 33 cm.).

Weights of adult Great Gray Owls range from approximately 1 1/2 pounds to 3 pounds (680 - 1360 grams). Female Great Gray Owls average about 10 - 15 percent larger than males.

Though Great Gray Owls are the largest of the North American owls, the Snowy Owl *(Nyctea scandiaca)* and the Great Horned Owl *(Bubo virginianus)* are heavier and apparently stronger.

The main visual characteristics of the Great Gray Owl are its size, the large rounded head (without "eartufts"), the large facial discs, and the conspicuous white "bow tie" markings on the throat. The bright yellow eyes are relatively smaller than with most other owls. The colour is generally a greyish-brown with much mottling and barring. The long loose feathers of the breast and tail are also a characteristic feature.

## DISTRIBUTION

Great Gray Owls are widely distributed across the northern forest of Canada, from north-western Quebec through northern Ontario, Manitoba, Saskatchewan, Alberta, British Columbia, and into the Northwest Territories and the Yukon. They also reside in the states of Minnesota, Montana, Wisconsin, Wyoming, Idaho, northern California, and Alaska.

They have been observed nesting near to the edge of the treeline at Churchill, Manitoba, and Winisk, Ontario in the north and as far south as Wisconsin and Yellowstone National Park in Wyoming. There are many records of nesting in northern Minnesota, southeastern Manitoba, and northern Alberta.

The winter range can be almost anywhere with a good food supply. In so-called "invasion" years when the owls wander southward in search of food, they appear along roadsides, in farmlands, near industrial areas, and even within cities and towns. During these movements they have been observed in the New England states, along the St. Lawrence River in Quebec, the Ottawa region, along the shore of Lake Ontario and around Sault Ste. Marie in Ontario, in northern Michigan, southern Minnesota, Wisconsin, southern Manitoba, and southern Alberta. A few have been seen in southwestern British Columbia including near Victoria.

The Great Gray Owl is also found in northern Eurasia where it is often called the Lapp Owl *(Strix nebulosa lapponica)*. There it varies somewhat in plumage details and behaviour but it is essentially the same owl.

## Habitat

In much of the range the Great Gray Owl prefers to nest in boggy areas of Black Spruce interspersed with Tamarack. It also frequently nests in Aspen forests. In the mountainous areas of the west it occupies Aspen and Coniferous forests of various types. Some populations prefer old mature forest with lots of broken snags. In the far north they nest in sparsely treed areas.

## NESTING SITES

This owl does not build its own nest. They usually will occupy an old nest of another species such as Goshawk, Raven, Red-tailed Hawk, or Broad-winged Hawk. Some of these may not be found within their preferred nesting habitat, which may lead to a compromise if they are to have a suitable nest platform.

Great Gray Owls also nest in the tops of broken off trees if such sites are available and if they are large enough. There is at least one record of them nesting on the ground in Canada.

Artificial nests, many of which have been constructed in Manitoba by Dr. Robert Nero and his associates, have proven to be very popular with Great Gray Owls. This was suggested by Dalton Muir of Ottawa, who had built artificial nests for Great Horned Owls in Ontario as early as the 1950's. One of the reasons for their success is that they are usually located in the habitat of preference for the owls. Structures built in Oregon, California, Wisconsin, Alberta, and British Columbia, have also been used by Great Gray Owls.

## EGGS

The usual clutch size is three. Some years they lay only two eggs, and in years when the adults are in good health and when food is plentiful, they may lay up to five. In extreme cases, as many as nine eggs have been observed, though it is thought to have been two females laying in one nest.

The eggs are more round than oval. They are off-white in colour, plain, with no obvious markings. Average measurements of the eggs are about 1 11/16 in. (43 mm.) across and 2 1/8 in. (54 mm.) in length. They have a smooth surface and a slight gloss; more of a lustre.

The eggs are usually laid at 2-day intervals and incubation begins with the first egg. The incubation period is 30 days and the chicks hatch out at 2-day intervals in the same sequence as they were laid.

## NESTLINGS

The nestlings are covered with white down when they hatch. Their eyes don't open until they are 5 days old. At 6 days, some grey appears in the shoulder areas and small sheaths of the primary feathers begin to show.

By the time they are 8 days of age, many grey feather sheaths are appearing in the wings and back. By this time their eyes are fully open, except when sleeping or dozing. At 10-11 days the owlets show considerable amounts of grey beneath the white down and the primary feathers are developed to a length of about one inch (25 mm.).

In 14 to 15 days they are beginning to look more like owls as the head fills out, the facial discs show more roundness, and their overall appearance becomes more greyish. At this point they also sit upright more of the time.

The third week shows significant changes in their plumage as the flight feathers lengthen, the body feathers fill out, and the white down begins to disappear. They spend much of their time preening. The young owls leave the nest as early as three weeks of age.

At this point they cannot fly, but they can flutter enough to slow a descent towards the ground. Often they end up on the ground itself and sometimes they crash-land in the branches of a tree. The fledglings are good climbers. Using their bill and their feet for grasping, and fluttering their wings for balance, they can climb up inclined tree trunks or logs to the safety of a branch or a stump.

## VOCALIZATIONS

The most familiar call of the Great Gray Owl is that of the adult male. It is described as "Whoo-whoo-whoo-hoo-hoo-hoo-hoo", being emphatic at the beginning and tapering off toward the end. There are usually six to ten syllables in quick succession. This is usually used as a courtship and a territorial song. Adult females sometimes give an almost identical call which is territorial in function.

There is another call used by the male and sometimes by the female which seems to indicate a warning (or annoyance) that something is intruding into their territory. It is a double note call "Hoo-oo, hoo-oo, hoo-oo, hoo-oo, hoo-oo", which is repeated a varying number of times and usually at a consistent intensity.

When the male brings prey to the nest, he often announces his arrival with a series of two or three hoots as he gets within a hundred metres or so. This often elicits an excited response from the female where she repeatedly gives loud demand calls and sometimes soft but emphatic hoots. Variations of these calls usually accompany the food exchange, which may take place on the nest itself or on a nearby branch or stump.

The most frequently heard call from the female is a food request call "ooo-uh", which rises to an emphatic second syllable. It varies from a soft infrequent utterence to a loud assertive demand. When food is scarce it has been recorded as often as every ten seconds. If the female and the nestlings have sufficient food this call may only be given once in 5 to 10 minutes. It is usually given right from the nest itself, but after the young are about 2 weeks of age it may be given from a nearby stump or branch. This call probably also serves as a locating call for the male to find the female.

Another call which is regularly made by the female at the nest is a mellow chatter, a staccato series of notes given rather softly as if meant only to communicate with the owlets. They will often be standing and looking down at the young when this call is used, and usually the young owls are making some sounds at the same time.

Usually about 3 days before the eggs hatch, a soft twittering sound will emanate from within the egg. Though it occurs at infrequent intervals it has a powerful effect on the attending female. At this point the female's attachment to the nest becomes much stronger, and she becomes more protective of the nest and its contents.

The most commonly heard call from the owlets after hatching is a thin, raspy "Zeeup" sound. This gets stronger as the young owls grow in size and continues to be issued even after they have left the nest and are sitting around in the forest. Owlets in the nest also give a number of weak notes and twittering sounds.

Adult Great Gray Owls of both sexes regularly use a single "Whoo" call at various levels of volume and degrees of emphasis throughout the year.

## FOOD

The favoured prey of the Great Gray Owl throughout most of its North American range is voles, particularly the Meadow Vole *(Microtus pennsylvanicus)*. They capture other species of small rodents, such as the Bog Lemming *(Synaptomys spp.)*, the Red-backed Vole *(Clethrionomys spp.)*, and a few mice and shrews. In the far northern regions they may even take other lemmings. In some of the Rocky Mountain regions, Pocket Gophers *(Thomomys spp.)* make up a significant portion of their diet.

Red Squirrels are captured occasionally, and there are a few records of them eating birds. A partially dismembered Spruce Grouse was found near the nest at The Pas, Manitoba in 1968 and it was presumed that the Great Gray Owl had killed it.

At one nest the owl was photographed with a Wood Frog as its prey proving that frogs are taken, though infrequently. There are also a few records of Great Gray Owls taking young Muskrats and young Snowshoe Hares.

## ABOUT THE PHOTOGRAPHY

The photographs which appear in the book span a period of almost thirty years, though most of them were made in the past ten. In the beginning, much of the nest photography was done with a Hasselblad 120 format camera. The majority of the work, however, was with 35 mm. Nikon cameras (FM-2, F-3, and F-4).

A motor drive was used for most of the flight photographs and hunting owls. At the nest, the motor drive was used sparingly, if at all. Flight shots were difficult as I estimated that the owls were travelling about 40 mph. (64 kph.) when on a long glide straight towards me. The most successful method of photographing was to focus the lens at a pre-determined distance and to shoot a sequence as the owl passed through the zone of focus.

Some of the flight photographs were made with a wide-angle lens and the owls were lured into camera range. In such cases a sequence of photographs was exposed and the best frames were selected.

Nest photography had its own requirements. Most of the photography and observation was done at man-made nests which were constructed for the benefit of the Great Gray Owls. The photographs in the book represent several such sites over the years. The first nest photography project was at The Pas, Manitoba, in the spring of 1968. A tower, using triangular television tower sections, was erected in the bush to a height of sixty feet. The camera was operated by remote control from the ground, which proved to be less than satisfactory as the compostion and actions in the photographs could not be judged properly from below. It was concluded that the photographer must be  at the camera position when doing this work.

The second filming and photography project was done in 1970. The location was the Roseau Bog in northern Minnesota, just across the border from South Junction, Manitoba. Dalton Muir drove from Ottawa (1,500 miles) and brought with him a wooden tower, which was essentially a double set of ladder sections with cross braces between. It was erected near the nest and to a height which placed the cameras slightly above the nest platform. After being secured

LEFT –*This owl was photographed at a distance of only a few feet after being lured to within camera range.* TOP RIGHT – *A Great Gray Owl about to take-off after being fed by the author along a roadside in rural Manitoba.* BOTTOM RIGHT – *The author and friend in a snowbank in eastern Manitoba.* (Photo by Jerry Anderson.)

LEFT –*The new aluminum tower and blind at a nest in eastern Manitoba in 1996. (Photo by Jerry Anderson.)*
TOP RIGHT – *Wooden tower and blind at the 1970 nest in Roseau Bog.*
BOTTOM RIGHT –*The author recording the sound of the male owl near a nest site. The microphone was within one inch of the owl's beak as he "hooted" into it.*

in place with guy wires, a blind was assembled on top. The photographer could climb up the inside, sit comfortably on the seat board, and make fine adjustments of the photography equipment as required. From this vantage point it was also possible to get more detailed observations of the birds' activities and to photograph them with more precision.

A tent was erected at some distance from the nest tree and we camped on location for the duration of the project. This tower was thirty-five feet high and it was removed from the site at the conclusion of the filming. No trace of our activity is ever left in the bush as we have a special appreciation for the beauty of these nesting locations.

The old wooden tower has been replaced by an aluminum tower which I had welded for me a few years ago. It has the advantage of being stronger and a bit lighter than the wooden one, and there are no slivers. Though the aluminum tower is somewhat lighter, we still usually require about three-hundred pounds of equipment for a nest photography project. Hauling all of this into a bog, a half-mile or more, through snow or knee-deep water requires much determination, not to mention the physical capability. As much resolution is required at the end of the project when everything has to be hauled out again, in the heat and the mosquitoes. The sheer joy of sharing that time with the owls makes all of the effort worth while.

Some of the nest photography has been done with short telephoto lenses and some of it with wide-angle lenses. Wherever the blind is situated, the tower and blind are installed slowly and very carefully so that the owls can get accustomed to our presence. At all times, the welfare of these magnificent birds is paramount.

Flash is used occasionally, to lighten harsh shadows in strong sunlight, and to provide illumination when photographing at dusk or at night. It is introduced slowly and is used sparingly. The owls do not seem to be bothered by electronic flash when it is used with consideration. The flash unit which was used is a Vivitar 283 with a Quantum power pack and a diffusion lens.

Until recently, I mostly used Kodachrome transparency films. In the past five years or so, I have utilized a number of different films ranging from 50 ISO/ASA slide films to 400 ISO/ASA colour negative films. Though I did use black and white films in the early years, I haven't done so in the last decade. In recent months I have been photographing wintering

Great Gray Owls with Kodak E-100 SW transparency film on bright days, and on dull days I have been using Fuji Provia 400 film. At the nest, I most recently used Fujicolor Super G Plus negative film (400 ISO/ASA) and Kodakchrome 64 transparency film. The main reason for using the 400 negative film was that I could get it processed on a daily basis so that I could make sure that everything was working out properly, especially balancing the flash to varying daylight conditions.

Some of the winter photographs of the Great Gray Owls in flight and perched have been made in the last few weeks before publication. This winter of 1996/97 has been a good one for observing Great Gray Owls, Northern Hawk Owls, and Snowy Owls in our region. On one day we saw 21 Great Grays, and another day, 18 Hawk Owls. Despite the deepest snow cover in many years, the Great Gray Owls are hunting the roadsides and farmlands and seem to be getting sufficient food. One evening, we watched an owl plunge into the snow and catch a vole twice in the space of two minutes. Though the text was finished, I could not resist spending three or four days per week watching and photographing the owls this winter. And I suppose that I will continue to do so for years to come.

# BIBLIOGRAPHY

Selected Bibliography
Prepared by James R. Duncan, PhD.

Alderson, G. (1960):
*The status of the Great Gray Owl
in Southern Oregon.*
Murrelet 41, 28.

Angell, Tony (1974):
*Owls.* University of Washington
Press, Seattle.

Armstrong, R.H. (1980):
*A guide to the birds of Alaska.*
Alaska Northwest Publishing
Co., Anchorage.

Bent, A.C. (1938):
*Life Histories of North American
Birds of Prey. Part 2:*
(U.S. National Museum Bulletin
No. 170.), Washington.

Bryan, T.; Forsman, E.D. (1987):
*Distribution, abundance, and
habitat of Great Gray Owls
in southcentral Oregon.*
Murrelet 68, 45-49.

Bull, E.L.; Duncan, J.R. (1993):
Great Gray Owl. In: *The Birds of
North America.* Vol. 41. The
Acedemy of Natural Sciences,
Philadelphia.

Burton, J.A. (Ed.)(1973):
*Owls of the World, Their Evolution,
Structure and Ecology.* E.P. Dutton,
N.Y.

Cadman, M.D.; Eagles, P.F.J.; Helleiner,
F.M. (1987):
*Atlas of the Breeding Birds of
Ontario.* University of Waterloo
Press, Waterloo, Ontario.

Duncan, J.R. (1987):
*Movement strategies, mortality, and
behaviour of radio-marked Great
Gray Owls in southeastern
Manitoba and northern Minnesota.*
Pages 101-107 in R.W. Nero, R.J.
Clark, R.J. Knapton, and R.H.
Hamre (Eds.). Biology and
Conservation of Northern Forest
Owls: Symposium Proceedings.
February 3-7; Winnipeg, Manitoba.
General Technical Report RM-142.
USDA Forest Service, Fort Collins,
Colorado.

Eckert, A.W. (1974):
*The Owls of North America.*
Doubleday & Co., Garden City,
N.Y.

Everett, M. (1977):
*A Natural History of Owls.*
Hamlyn Publishing Group, London.

Fortin, L.; Savard, J.; Aubert, C. (1983):
*Etudes des population d'oiseaux de
la region Quebec.* Club des
Ornithologues du Quebec,
Charlesburg, PQ.

Franklin, A.B. (1988):
*Breeding biology of the Great Gray
Owl in southeastern Idaho and
northwestern Wyoming.* The
Condor 90, 689-696.

Godfrey, W.E. (1986):
*The Birds of Canada*, revised
edition. National Museum of
Canada, Bulletin 203, Ottawa.

Guiguet, C.J. (1978):
*The Birds of British Columbia* (7)
Owls. K.M. MacDonald, Victoria,
B.C.

Harris, W.C. (1984):
*Great Gray Owls in Saskatchewan*
(1974-1983). Blue Jay 42 (3),
152-160.

Houston, S. (1957):
*The Great Gray Owl in
Saskatchewan.* Blue Jay 15,
150-153.

Johnsgard, P.A. (1988):
*North American Owls.* Smithsonian
Institution Press, Washington.

Merkel, K.J. (1989):
*Wisconsin's first documented
nesting of Great Gray Owls.*
Passenger Pigeon 51 (2).

Mikkola, Heimo (1983):
*Owls of Europe.* Buteo Books,
Vermillion, South Dakota.

Muir, Dalton (1972):
*At the nest of a Great Gray Owl.*
Nature Canada, 1, 20-22.

Nero, R.W. (1986):
*The Great Gray Owl: Phanton
of the Northern Forest.*
Smithsonian Institution Press,
Washington, D.C. (Photographs by
Robert R. Taylor)

Quinton, M.S. (1988):
*Ghost of the Forest, the Great Gray
Owl.* Northland Press, Flagstaff,
Arizona.

Semenchuck, G.P. (Ed.) (1992):
*The atlas of the breeding birds of
Alberta.* Federation of Alberta
Naturalists, Edmonton.

Sparks, J.; Soper, T. (1970):
*Owls: Their Natural and Unnatural
History.* Taplinger Publishing Co.,
N.Y.

Voous, K.H. (1988):
*Owls of the northern hemisphere.*
MIT Press, Cambridge, Mass.

Walker, L.W. (1974):
*The Book of Owls.* A.A. Knopf,
N.Y.

---

*Profiles of Nature
The Great Gray Owl*

by Robert R. Taylor
and Dalton Muir

Available in VHS Video Cassette
(24 minutes in length)

May be ordered from:

KEG Productions
(Ellis Enterprises)
Toronto, Ontario, Canada
Tel: (416) 924-2186
Fax: (416) 924-6115